Full STEAM Ahead!

Math Matters

Building Tens with My Friends

Adrianna Morganelli

CRABTREE
PUBLISHING COMPANY
WWW.CRABTREEBOOKS.COM

Title-Specific Learning Objectives:

Readers will:

- Identify ways to add ones to make a bundle of ten.
- Count objects in groups of ten and in groups of tens and ones.
- Make connections between math ideas in the text to understand how ones and tens are related.

High-frequency words (grade one)	Academic vocabulary
and, are, do, make, see, the, you, with	bundle, count, ones, tens

Before, During, and After Reading Prompts:

Activate Prior Knowledge and Make Predictions:
Have children read the title and look at the cover images. Ask children:

- What do you see in the picture? What are the children doing?
- Have you ever used blocks in math class?
- What do you know about counting with tens?

During Reading:
After reading page 6, stop and ask children:

- What do you notice about the word "bundle"? (It is in bold type.)
- Do you know what a bundle is? (Children can use the pictures and words on the page to help.)

Direct children to look at page 22: Words to Know. Read the definition for the word "bundle." Ask children:

- How do the definition, the words on page 6, and the pictures help us understand what a bundle is?
- Encourage children to use the "Words to Know" page as a tool to support comprehension.

After Reading:
Have children practice making bundles of ten using colored blocks. They must use at least two different colors. Invite children to record the number sentence that describes their bundle. They can also work in groups to add their bundles together. They can use the number sentences below:

___ + ___ = 10   10 + ___ + ___ = ___

Author: Adrianna Morganelli

Series Development: Reagan Miller

Editor: Janine Deschenes

Proofreader: Melissa Boyce

STEAM Notes for Educators: Reagan Miller and Janine Deschenes

Guided Reading Leveling: Publishing Solutions Group

Cover, Interior Design, and Prepress: Samara Parent

Photo research: Janine Deschenes and Samara Parent

Production coordinator: Katherine Berti

Photographs:
iStock: pacopole: p. 9 (top); Antagain: p. 9 (bottom); AYImages: p. 18 (left); ivanastar: p. 19; Maica: p. 21 (top)
All other photographs by Shutterstock

Library and Archives Canada Cataloguing in Publication

Morganelli, Adrianna, 1979-, author
Building tens with my friends / Adrianna Morganelli.

(Full STEAM ahead!)
Includes index.
Issued in print and electronic formats.
ISBN 978-0-7787-6230-0 (hardcover).--
ISBN 978-0-7787-6291-1 (softcover).--ISBN 978-1-4271-2269-8 (HTML)

1. Counting--Juvenile literature. 2. Addition--Juvenile literature. I. Title.

QA113.M69 2019   j513.2'11   C2018-906204-5
C2018-906205-3

Library of Congress Cataloging-in-Publication Data

Names: Morganelli, Adrianna, 1979- author.
Title: Building tens with my friends / Adrianna Morganelli.
Description: New York, New York : Crabtree Publishing Company, [2019] | Series: Full STEAM ahead! | Includes index.
Identifiers: LCCN 2018056801 (print) | LCCN 2018059628 (ebook) | ISBN 9781427122698 (Electronic) | ISBN 9780778762300 (hardcover : alk. paper) | ISBN 9780778762911 (pbk. : alk. paper)
Subjects: LCSH: Counting--Juvenile literature. | Addition--Juvenile literature. | Arithmetic--Juvenile literature.
Classification: LCC QA113 (ebook) | LCC QA113 .M677 2019 (print) | DDC 513.2/11--dc23
LC record available at https://lccn.loc.gov/2018056801

Printed in the U.S.A./042019/CG20190215

Table of Contents

Crabtree Publishing Company
www.crabtreebooks.com 1-800-387-7650

In Canada: We acknowledge the financial support of the Government of Canada through the Book Publishing Industry Development Program (BPIDP) for our publishing activities.

Published in Canada
Crabtree Publishing
616 Welland Ave.
St. Catharines, Ontario
L2M 5V6

Published in the United States
Crabtree Publishing
PMB 59051
350 Fifth Avenue, 59th Floor
New York, New York 10118

Published in the United Kingdom
Crabtree Publishing
Maritime House
Basin Road North, Hove
BN41 1WR

Published in Australia
Crabtree Publishing
Unit 3 – 5 Currumbin Court
Capalaba
QLD 4157

Counting Beads

Oscar and Anika are using beads to make bracelets. "How many beads do we have?" Anika asks.

Oscar and Anika want to **count** the beads. Counting lets them find the number of beads.

We use numbers to count. We start with one, then name the numbers in order.

How many yellow beads do you see? How many red beads do you see?

Bundles of Ten

Oscar counts ten beads.
Ten is a **bundle** of ten **ones**.

Bundles of ten ones are called **tens**.

Anika thinks it will take too long to count all of the beads. “Let’s count the rest of the beads in tens,” she says.

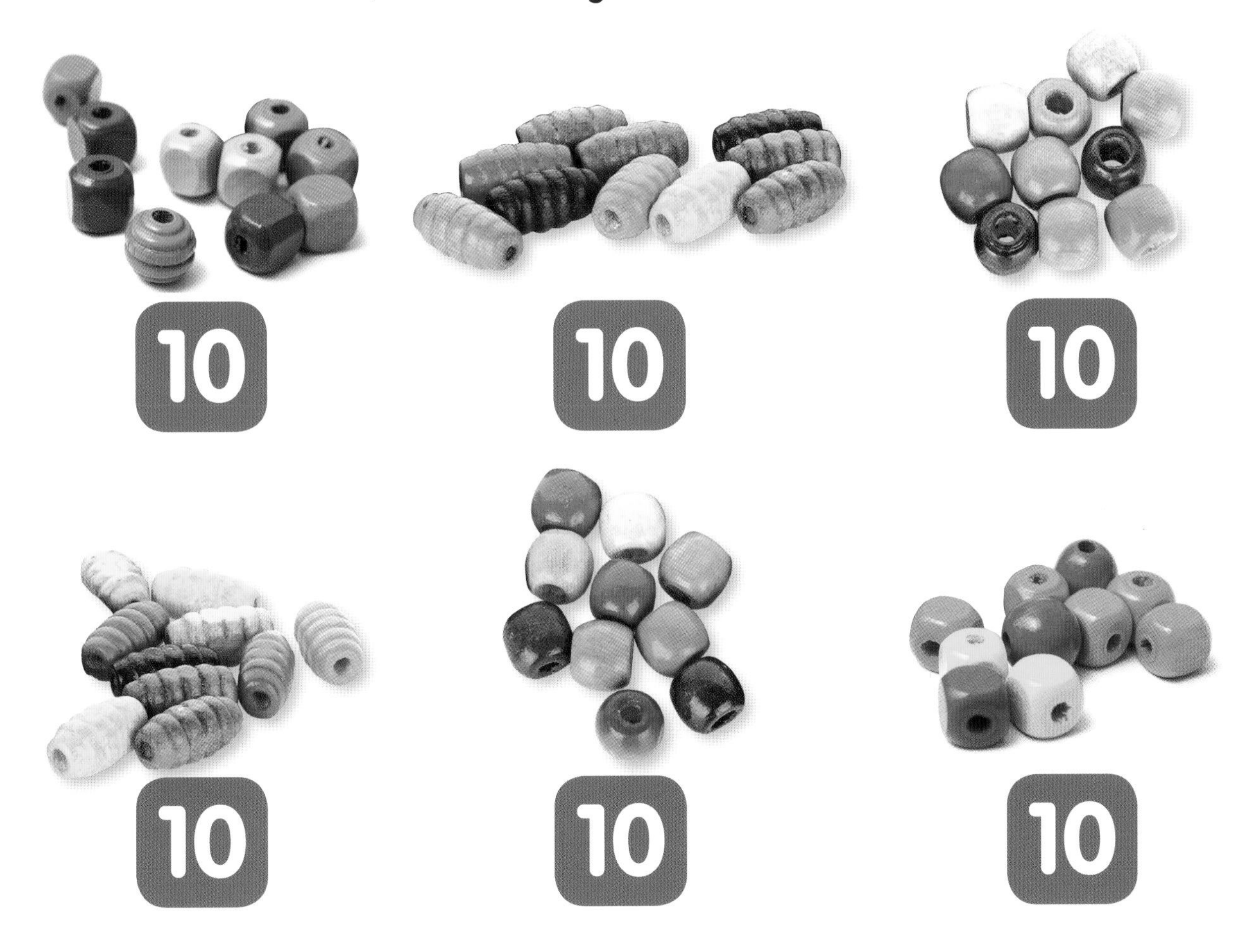

There are six bundles of ten beads. That makes 60 beads.

Counting in Tens

Counting in tens is quicker than counting in ones. We can count large numbers by adding bundles of tens together.

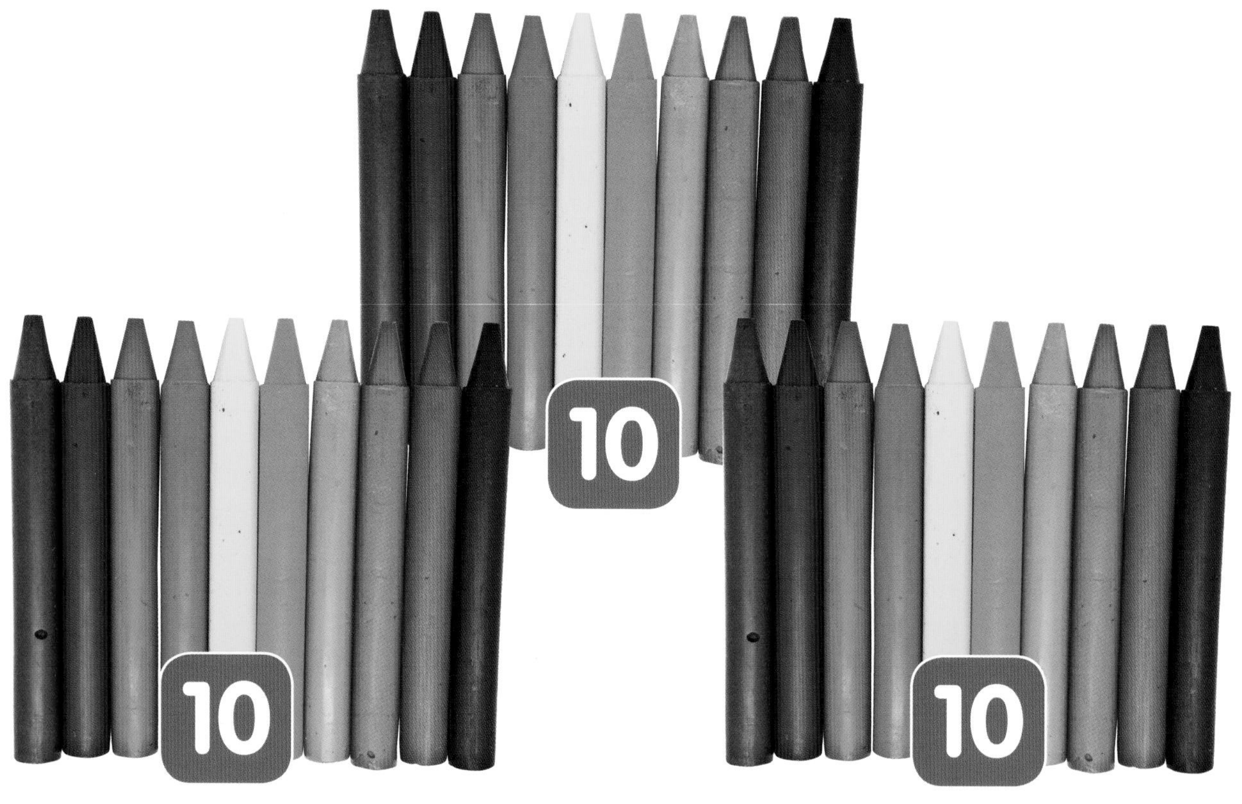

There are three bundles of ten crayons. That makes 30 crayons.

How many strawberries are there? Count in tens to find out.

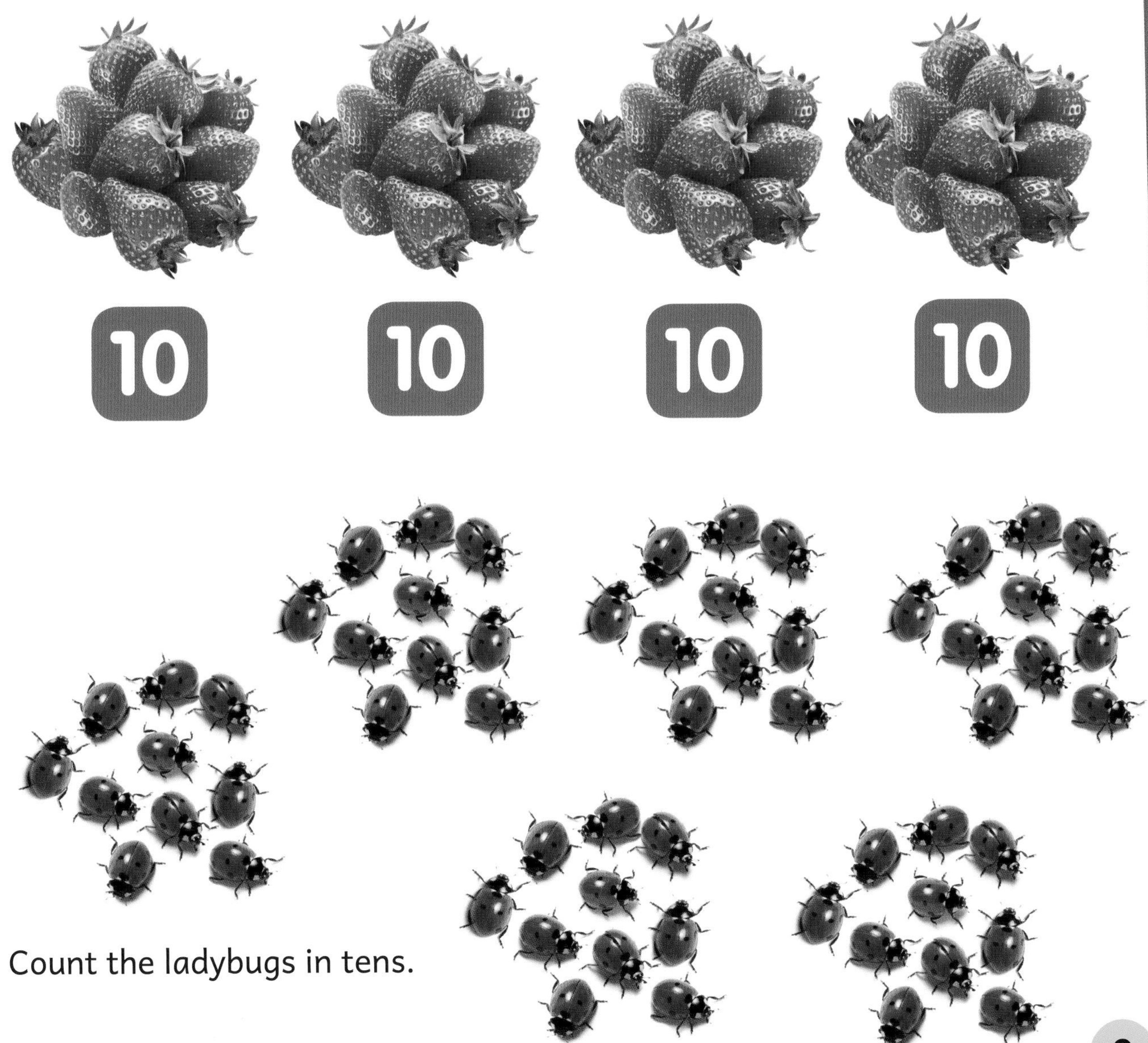

Count the ladybugs in tens.

How Many to Ten?

We can make bundles of tens in many ways. Anika makes eight cupcakes. She wonders how many more she needs to make ten.

Oscar gives Anika two more cupcakes. Eight plus two makes ten.

$8 + 2 = 10$

3 + _ = 10

Anika makes three more cupcakes. How many more does she need to make ten?

Toss to Ten

Anika, Oscar, and their friends play a hoop toss game. Players get one point for each hoop they throw around the cone.

The first team to get ten points wins!

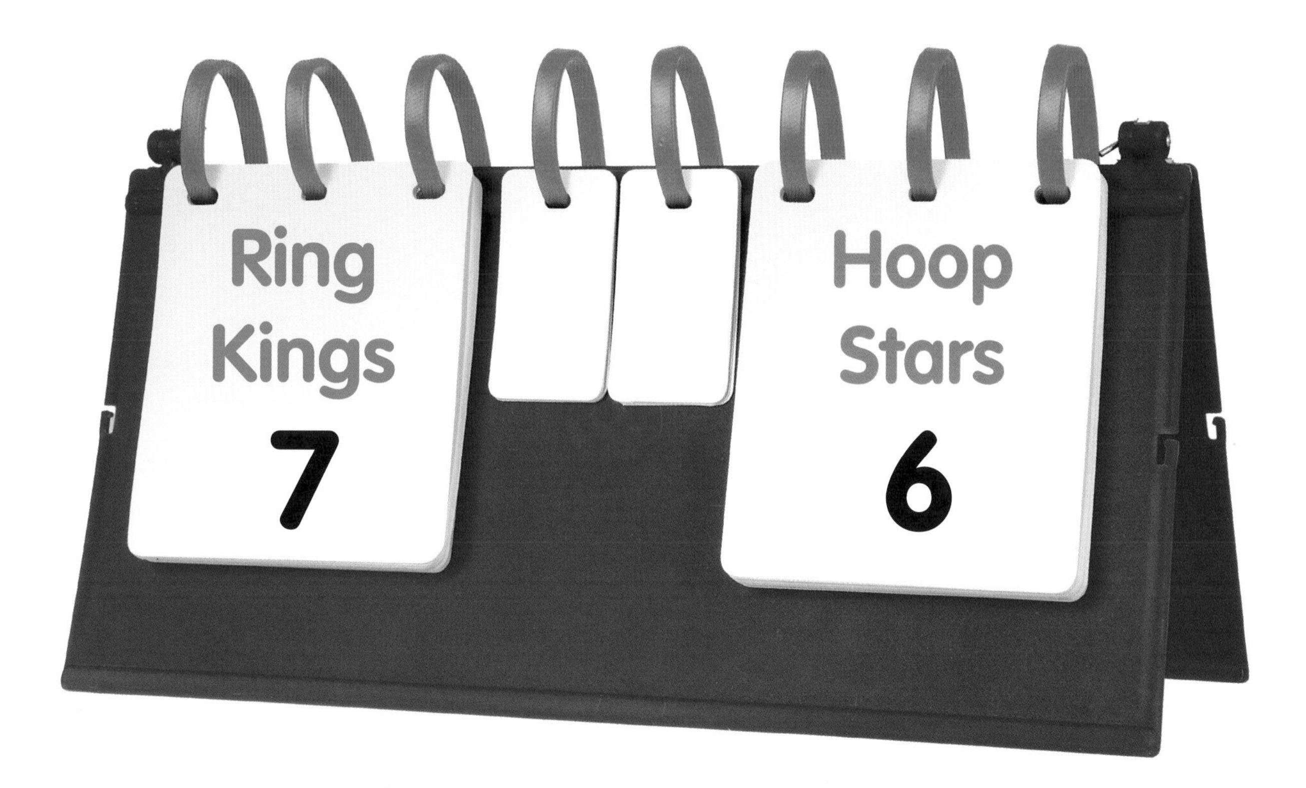

How many more points
do the Ring Kings need to win?

The Hoop Stars score four more points.
Do they have enough points to win the game?

Making Tens

Help Anika and Oscar make tens.

1 + _ = 10

Anika has one soccer ball. How many more does she need to make ten?

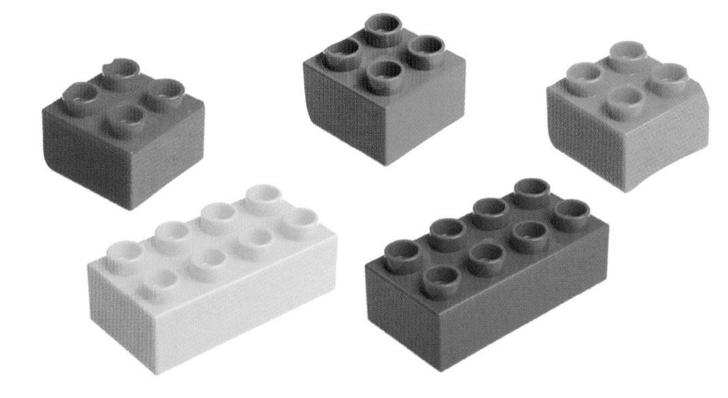

5 + _ = 10

Oscar has five blocks. How many more does he need to make ten?

How many more marbles do Anika and Oscar need to make three bundles of tens?

Tens and Ones

Each number from 11 to 19 is a bundle of ten with a number left over. The leftover numbers are ones.

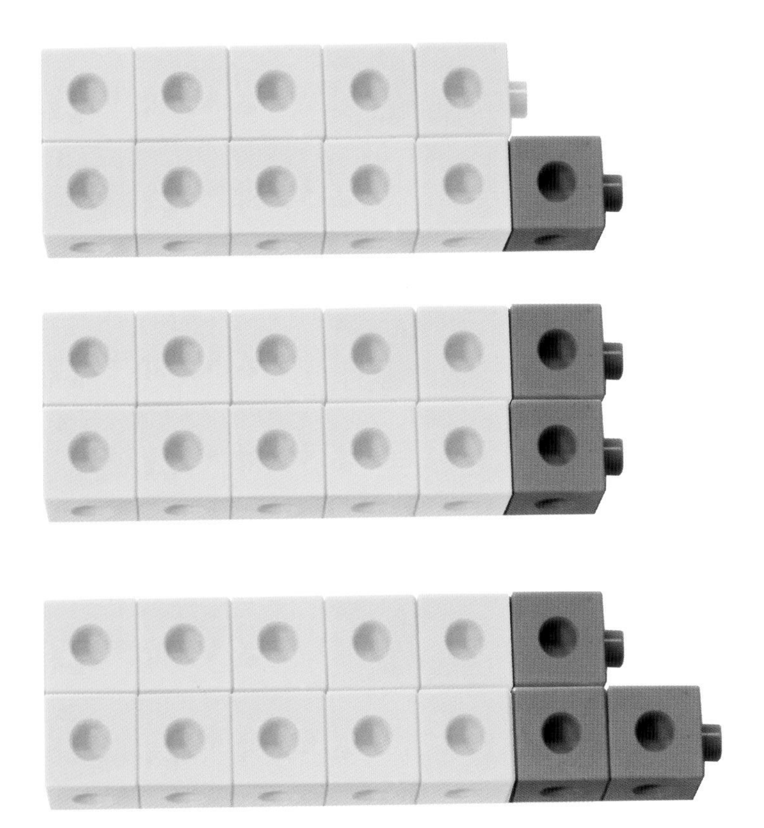

11 is one bundle of ten and one left over.

12 is one bundle of ten and two left over.

13 is one bundle of ten and three left over.

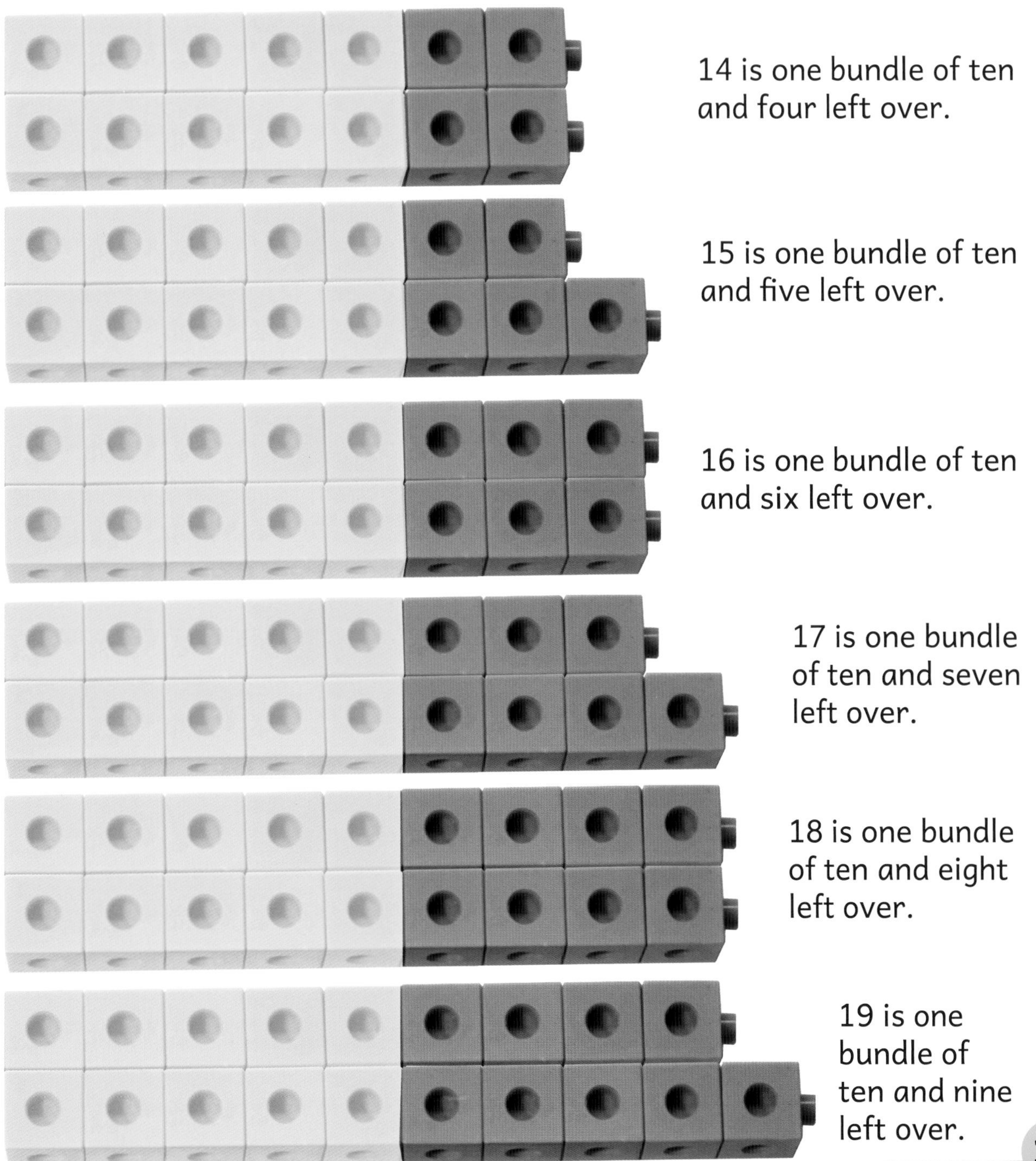

14 is one bundle of ten and four left over.

15 is one bundle of ten and five left over.

16 is one bundle of ten and six left over.

17 is one bundle of ten and seven left over.

18 is one bundle of ten and eight left over.

19 is one bundle of ten and nine left over.

How Many Ones Left?

This box can hold ten crayons.
How many ones are left over?

How many crayons are there in all?

Oscar helps his mother pick up sticks in the backyard.

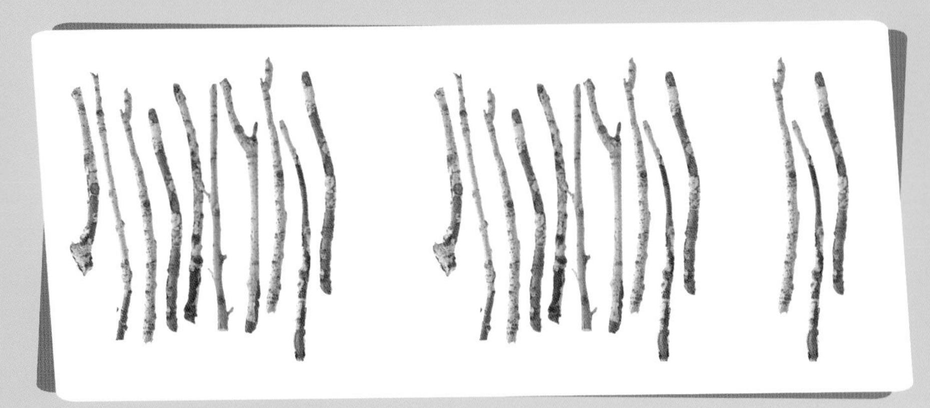

Oscar collected 23 sticks. He has two tens. There are three sticks left. He has three ones.

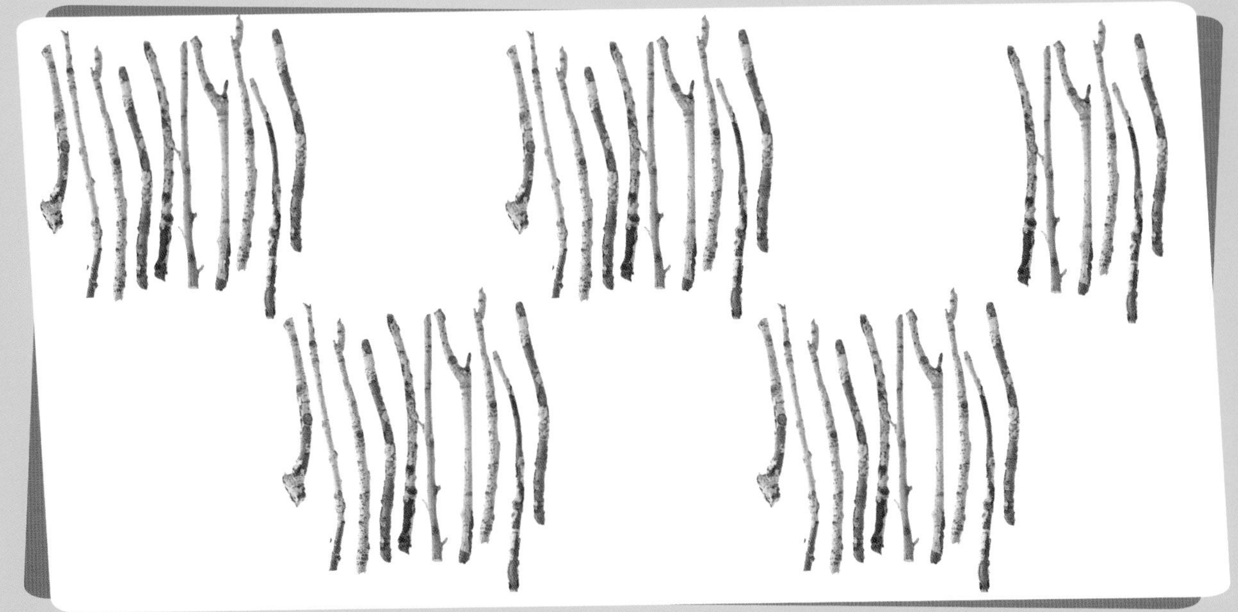

Oscar's mother collected 46 sticks.
How many tens does she have? How many ones?

Bundles at the Beach

Anika and her grandfather pick up **trash** at the beach. They put empty bottles in bags.

Ten bottles fill each bag. How many bottles did Anika and her grandfather collect?

Anika likes to **collect** seashells.
She and her grandfather look for new shells.

Count Anika's seashells. How many bundles of tens did she collect?
How many ones are left over?

Words to Know

bundle [BUHN-dl] noun
Objects put together in a group, such as a ten

collect [kuh-LEKT] verb
To gather together objects from different places, often to create a collection or larger group

count [kount] verb To add to find the total number of objects in a group

ones [wuhns] noun
Number for single objects or units

tens [tens] noun Groups of ten ones

trash [trash] noun
Things people throw away

A noun is a person, place, or thing.

A verb is an action word that tells you what someone or something does.

An adjective is a word that tells you what something is like.

Index

About the Author

Adrianna Morganelli is an editor and writer who has worked with Crabtree Publishing on countless book titles. She is currently working on a children's novel.

To explore and learn more, enter the code at the Crabtree Plus website below.

www.crabtreeplus.com/fullsteamahead

Your code is:
fsa20

STEAM Notes for Educators

Full STEAM Ahead is a literacy series that helps readers build vocabulary, fluency, and comprehension while learning about big ideas in STEAM subjects. *Building Tens with My Friends* helps readers identify and answer questions about ideas related to basic place value and addition. The STEAM activity below helps readers extend the ideas in the book to build their skills in math and engineering.

A Structure of Ten

Children will be able to:

- Show their math knowledge by compiling and identifying bundles of tens.
- Use a bundle of ten objects to build a structure that fits specific criteria.

Materials

- "A Structure of Ten" Worksheet
- Yardstick, meter stick, ruler, or other measuring tool (educator's choice)
- Project materials including recycled boxes, cans, and bottles, pencils, coins, glue, tape, rubber bands, craft sticks, etc.

Guiding Prompts

After reading *Building Tens with My Friends*, ask:

- How many ones are in a bundle of ten?
- Why is it useful to group objects into tens when counting?

Activity Prompts

Explain to children that they will create a structure from one bundle of ten objects.

Review the criteria for the structure.

- Each structure must be as tall as one yardstick (one meter stick). (Choose appropriate goal for children.)
- Each structure must be made of one bundle of ten (in total, ten objects).
- The bundle of ten needs to be made of three different types of objects.
- Each group writes a number sentence to describe their bundle of ten, such as: 3 cans + 2 tissue boxes + 5 craft sticks = 10

Have children form groups of three to four. Each group builds a structure. Each child fills in their own "A Structure of Ten" Worksheet.

Have each group present their structure and the number sentence that describes it. Test each structure by measuring it. Discuss what worked well and what could be improved. Children can then revise their structure if it did not meet the criteria.

Extensions

- Have children examine two other groups' structures. Have them write and present number sentences that describe the other groups' bundles of ten.

To view and download the worksheets, visit **www.crabtreebooks.com/resources/printables** or **www.crabtreeplus.com/fullsteamahead** and enter the code **fsa20**.